HOW TO PLAY THE FIFE

A Beginner's Guide to Learning the Basics, Reading Music, and Playing Songs with Audio Recordings

Text Copyright © Lightbulb Publishing

All rights reserved. No part of this guide may be reproduced in any form without permission in writing from the publisher except in the case of brief quotations embodied in critical articles or reviews.

Legal & Disclaimer

The information contained in this book and its contents is not designed to replace or take the place of any form of medical or professional advice; and is not meant to replace the need for independent medical, financial, legal or other professional advice or services, as may be required. The content and information in this book has been provided for educational and entertainment purposes only.

The content and information contained in this book has been compiled from sources deemed reliable, and it is accurate to the best of the Author's knowledge, information, and belief. However, the Author cannot guarantee its accuracy and validity and cannot be held liable for any errors and/or omissions. Further, changes are periodically made to this book as and when needed. Where appropriate and/or necessary, you must consult a professional (including but not limited to your doctor, attorney, financial advisor or such other professional advisor) before using any of the suggested remedies, techniques, or information in this book.

Upon using the contents and information contained in this book, you agree to hold harmless the Author from and against any damages, costs, and expenses, including any legal fees potentially resulting from the application of any of the information provided by this book. This disclaimer applies to any loss, damages or injury caused by the use and application, whether directly or indirectly, of any advice or information presented, whether for breach of contract, tort, negligence, personal injury, criminal intent, or under any other cause of action.

You agree to accept all risks of using the information presented in this book.

You agree that by continuing to read this book, where appropriate and/or necessary, you shall consult a professional (including but not limited to your doctor, attorney, or financial advisor or such other advisor as needed) before using any of the suggested remedies, techniques, or information in this book.

Table of Contents

Chapter 1: Introduction..1

Chapter 2: Navigating the Fife and Basic Care..........................7

Chapter 3: Understanding Music Notes and Rhythm 19

Chapter 4: How to Play Notes on the Fife 41

Chapter 5: Playing Your First Songs 47

Chapter 6: Intermediate Fife Techniques 61

Chapter 7: Conclusion - Bringing It All Together 71

Throughout this book there are musical examples and audio recordings to follow along with on your journey to learn how to play the saxophone.

Whenever you see the following outline:

> **Listening Sound File #1**
> Listen to a written D note on the fife.
> (This note is written as D, but is sounding as a real B♭ note.

Please follow along with the recordings at the Sound Cloud link below or search on Sound Cloud for "How to Play the Fife".

https://soundcloud.com/jason_randall/sets/how-to-play-the-fife?utm_source=clipboard&utm_medium=text&utm_campaign=social_sharing

Chapter 1
Introduction

Congratulations on deciding to learn the fife!

The fife is an excellent place to start for ambitious learners. It is reputably one of the more difficult woodwinds to master. The journey to learn this historical instrument will not only be fulfilling in itself, but can also open many doors to other woodwinds and brass. This book will teach you how to get comfortable with a classic 6-hole fife, as well as how to be comfortable reading simple music notation to continuously learn new songs. You'll learn basic techniques and be introduced to intermediate techniques to keep yourself developing. Also in this book are examples of classic litanies and tunes for the fife so you can be piping away in no time.

The Importance of Historical Context

Musical instruments are interesting, because the tone and timbre are inextricably linked to historical context. As a player, we need to know where our instruments come from, because it may cue up many ideas from the mere sounding of it. A choir or an organ register in the mind as church or gospel music. The bagpipes immediately signal images of Scotland. And the fife primarily has a deeply rooted history with military regiments.

Composers tend to use the history of instruments to convey certain messages. Before moving on, get acquainted with a brief history of this widely used instrument.

Early History of the Fife

The fife has several centuries of history behind it. This includes how it was used and also how it was developed into more complex renditions. However, contemporary fifes have still not become more popular than the original 6-hole design.

Fife comes from the German word "pfeife", meaning pipe. The instrument is a simple pipe structure with coverable holes that allow the passage of air to be changed in frequency. Its simple design as a transverse wind instrument (or an instrument receiving air from the side to make noise) is similar to the flute, and musicologists have traced it back to being the original piccolo.

The first known fifes were present in medieval Europe. All social classes of the dark ages enjoyed fifes. They were often used in chamber ensembles during dance parties. But most people connote the sound of the fife to such militant endeavors as the Civil War. Since the Crusades in the 12th century, the fife has garnered the reputation as a military instrument, most often accompanied by marching drums. Switzerland and Germany are most notable for having used the fife in infantry units as early as the 15th century.

And even after the Crusades, furthering the reputation as a military instrument, most armies throughout Europe in the 18th century introduced the rank of Fife Major, analogous to Drum Major. When the Revolutionary War came around, both the British and American armies were using the fife to signify battle or spur on duties in camps.

When colonialism spread across New England, the fife persisted in popularity. It was the predominant instrument in the colonial

Introduction

period, even more widely used than orchestral instruments like the piano, violin, or cello. This, along with its history as a military instrument, also made it notorious in the Civil War for marching infantry. Even after five centuries, the fife was still being played alongside drums to signify an attack was looming just over the hill. Several historical accounts claim that the shrill pitch of the instrument could be heard over artillery fire for more than three-mile distances. Talk about dynamics!

The fife was rarely seen in ensembles during colonial years. This was mostly due to not many people knowing how to play in tune with other members. No one took the time to train infantry members on how to play anything but folk tunes, therefore defaulting instrumentalists to play solely with percussion. Indeed, making a finely tuned noise on the instrument is still challenging for beginners. Its range is one of the highest, and higher frequencies have less forgiveness in terms of precision. This makes playing the instrument much easier in a solo environment, and much more finicky when trying to harmonize with other high-range instruments.

In addition, the modern frequency definition of the note concert A didn't come about until 1939. Concert A is the internationally standardized frequency of 440hz. It is the note used for 99% of music, from recordings of pop, R and B, and rock to symphonies and opera. It might be most recognizable when watching an orchestra tune their instruments before beginning to play. However, before the standardization in 1939 musicians relied on more subjective variations of frequency, which made the imprecision of the fife's higher range even less tamable. Traditionally, fifes tend to sound a concert A at 443hz or 446hz, which means it is naturally a bit sharper in character, though still perceivably in tune by most ears.

Various Instances

Historically, the fife has appeared in various cultures and influenced folk music differently. Colonialism in America wasn't the only instance of introduction for the fife. Portuguese military brought the musical instrument over to the Brazilians in the 16th and 17th centuries.

The fife has been merely a part of extensive history. Due to the fact that it is barely distinguishable from ancient flutes, it is arguable that the history of these woodwinds can be traced to 50,000 years ago. The Neanderthal Flute is a 1995 archaeological find in Divje Babe, an area in Slovenia. This relic is the most ancient instrument catalogued by humanity. It was carved from the bones of a cave bear, and its simple design makes it still playable today. Other flutes of prehistoric origin included versions from vulture-bone and mammoth ivory.

Later History of the Fife

Throughout the 20th century, the fife has maintained a strong connotation to folk music and military application. The Company of Fifers and Drummers, located in eastern Connecticut, celebrates the instrument with a museum in Ivoryton, and continue to perform marching fife and drum corps for entertainment purposes.

The Marines were the last corps to retire the fifer position in the US. However, Britain still retains fife and drum corps, which

Introduction

mostly serve in parades and memorials. During World War II, Germany had fifers in most regiments.

Despite (and sometimes even due to) this bellicose legacy, the fife remains an applicable instrument in composition. Recent developments have made this instrument more in-tune and more capable of playing every note on the standardized musical spectrum. As we'll see later, every note within a three-octave range is achievable, but in general the fife uses only three major scales.

The advent of a fife with seven holes was made to help facilitate lower D# notes, which is only achievable on 6-hole fifes by half-covering the furthest hole with all others covered. Manufacturers and designers went even further by creating both 10-hole and 11-hole fifes. These are more similar to flutes and also more capable of making purer toned notes outside of the main three scales the fife is known for.

After seeing the history of the fife, it's easy to understand why most associate it with military corps. This is important to be aware of. Naturally, though, music can be more than a statement. It can be a means of expression, sublimation, or creativity. It's important to remember that the fife was originally used for entertainment before being dowsed in connotations of warfare. So, as a player, use this instrument however you'd like to, and remember that since the dawn of our species, music has ultimately been the most incredible way we have expressed ourselves without any need for words.

Chapter 2
Navigating the Fife and Basic Care

Topics Covered:

- How to hold the fife

- Getting a sound out of it

- Tuning

- Fife pitch considerations and a note on this book's audio

- Taking care of the fife

- Taking breaks

Your first fife should come from the manufacturer all set to begin. It's a simple design, and you won't have to make any adjustments before getting started. However, if it's your first time playing a woodwind instrument, it will take some patience.

How to Hold the Fife

The fife is a side-blown instrument. It will be pointing out to the right side of your face from your perspective, running parallel to your lips. This means when you hold it up to your face, the six finger holes will be to your right.

Your left hand will be closest to your face, the palm facing you. The index, middle, and ring finger of the left hand should be positioned to cover the first three holes of the fife nearest your face.

picture/diagram of holding fife with just left hand

The right hand will take care of the remaining three holes, again using the index, middle, and ring. The important difference is that the right hand's palm will be facing away from your face, while the left always faces toward you. With this finger positioning in mind, remember which fingers go to which hole.

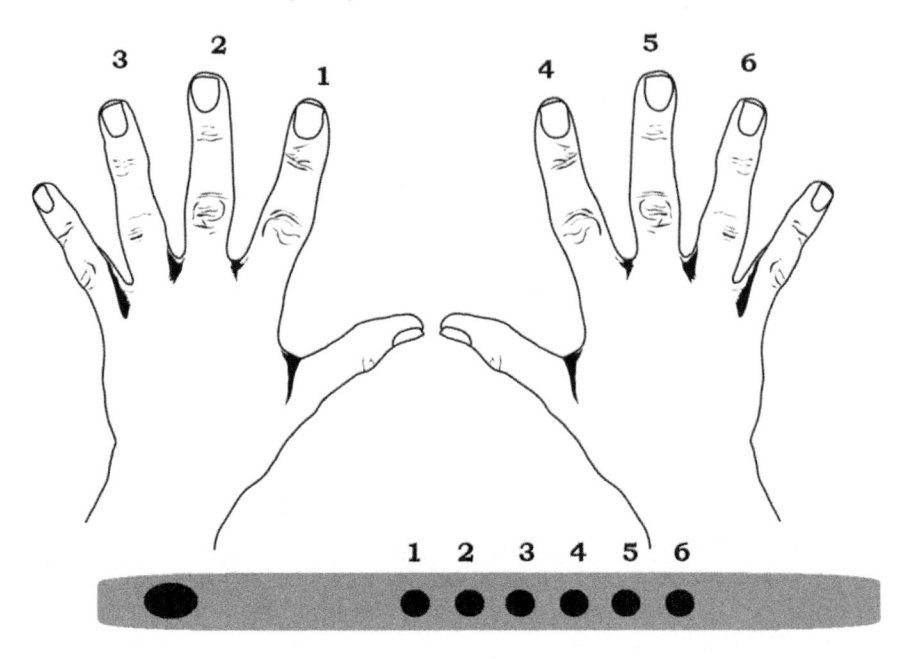

You might wonder what to do with your pinkies. Different players have different ways of using their pinky and thumb, which ultimately changes the pressure on the finger holes. There is room for adjustment based on comfort, but it's important to keep in mind that the thumbs and pinkies might be the only digits supporting the fife when all holes are open.

Several fife players are most comfortable with placing the right hand's thumb directly below the fourth hole, meaning it is lined up under your right index finger. Players also tend to lay their right pinky flat across the top surface, creating a firm pressure downward. With that downward pressure, the blowhole can be levered upward to the mouth to create firm positioning. With this positioning, the right hand will get a little tired from the awkward strain. But an important way to check is to see that you're holding the fife securely with only your right hand. If you can firmly and confidently hold the fife with solely your right hand, you'll be able to change fingering much more easily. Lastly about the right hand, recall that some fifes have a seventh hole. In that case it would negate this positioning. Flautists who are learning the fife also get confused by this pinky position, because the pinky is used to press another key on the flute. But this is not true with ordinary fifes.

The left hand can counter the levered pressure from the right hand by securing a firm fixed position against your bottom lip. Most players' left thumbs are not directly under the index finger. It will be almost pointing to the left, with the left side of it touching the bottom surface of the fife. The left pinky is much less important than the right pinky and can find its most comfortable position. Most players position their left pinkies with the tip against the side of the fife, lined up with the right thumb and index finger, but not getting in the way of either.

The blowhole, which is the biggest hole of the fife, should be facing upward and ready to press against your bottom lip. Obviously, this is the entrance where your breaths will enter the instrument from a down-blown position.

The last thing to look for with holding your fife is its horizontal position. When held properly, the fife should be absolutely parallel to the floor. This will stretch the right shoulder muscles, feeling unnatural at first. This exact horizontal position might be trying at the beginning, but it will increase the volume of your playing and make hitting notes easiest as the wind from your mouth will be entering at the perfect angle.

Posture

Music teachers from every time period everywhere have promulgated good posture with any instrument. With wind instruments, this consideration is even more important because it affects the quality of airflow.

The best way to ensure proper posture is to stand while playing. Standing in front of a mirror will also help see if you're holding the instrument well enough, keeping it horizontal, balanced, and pointing to the right. If you prefer to sit, it is crucial to sit up straight and avoid slouching, allowing the lungs to expand and your face to be in line with your body, confirming solid position against the lip. Again, if you can't seem to make a sound while sitting, it very well might be because you'd be better off standing.

Getting a Sound out of the Fife

Now that you know how to hold the fife, the next step is knowing the relationship between your mouth and the blowhole. The fife should be positioned in the middle of your mouth, so the middle of the blowhole aligns with your philtrum. Place it under the bottom lip so the air coming from between your lips doesn't go completely inside the blowhole but so some the breath is scathed across the edge of the hole.

Your lips need to be pressed tightly together, creating the smallest opening you can achieve with a nearly closed mouth. A good tip to test this is to place a dry piece of rice between closed lips and blow until the rice pops out. This tight-lipped way of blowing at a controlled angle is called embouchure. To practice your embouchure, you don't need a fife. Professional fife players can achieve three octaves from an empty bottle. This will take time to get good at, but the same concept applies with blowing into a bottle as with across the fife's blowhole.

When trying to get your first sounds from the fife, start by covering all the finger holes. You might only achieve faint sounds, but by barely rolling the fife back and forth against the fixed position under your lip, the wind will catch more conducive angles. Find the angle at which sounds are crispest. Rolling in flattens the pitch, while rolling away sharpens the pitch. This flattening and sharpening won't change the pitch itself, just the quality of the pitch.

Tuning

Your fife should arrive pre-tuned. But it's important to know the mechanics of how to fine tune your instrument. At the end near the blowhole, there is usually a cork or a metal joint for tuning the fife. This is fit snugly in place, but the distance it enters and blocks the bore of the instrument further fine tunes the pitch. The more the cork is pushed in, the sharper it will be. Conversely, the more the cork is pulled out, the flatter the pitch will be. The cork should never be passed the edge of the blowhole.

If the fife is new, there shouldn't be any need to change the position of the cork or tuning joint. However, if you have an older fife, the cork may have worn out. Positioning older corks might break them and make the instrument incapable of producing a good sound. If it's slightly out of tune but the cork looks brittle, it's best to leave it alone and practice solo. The pitch may not be perfect, but it will be uniformly out of tune which won't be noticeable at all when playing alone.

For those more mechanically inclined, you can make new corks with old wine corks. Shave the new cork down to just barely larger than the fife's tube, then shape it with sandpaper to fit snugly using petroleum jelly. Adjust the cork until blowing into it makes the desired in-tune pitch.

Considerations About Pitch

The fife is a transposing instrument. Transposition means the note that the player plays from the written sheet music is not the same note as what we hear. Musical notes are not relative. There is an international standardization of what constitutes every note. Concert A is 440hz. An octave is double the frequency, so an A above concert A would register at 880hz. But transposed instruments are not playing an A at all when they read an A off the sheet music. This is always true, because transposition was created so the players could more easily read their notes on the staff.

If you are familiar with transposition, then don't make the mistake of assuming the same principles apply to the traditional 6-hole fife! Please be aware that the fife is not a traditionally transposed instrument. For the vast majority of instruments, the traditional method for naming and transposing instruments is based on what sounds when a written C note is played. For example, the trumpet is a B♭ instrument because it plays the actual note of B♭ when the written note is a C. The same is true for all orchestral instruments.

But the fife is different!

The fife is based on the note of D. And it is a traditionally a B♭ instrument. This means that, unlike the trumpet, a sounding B♭ correlates to a written D. Every time you read a D note, you are actually playing a B♭. That means that every time you read a C note, you are actually playing an A♭ note. This is a hugely important difference to be aware of. All other instruments with this transposition would be called an A♭ instrument, because the written note would be C. But the fife is based not on C, but on D, so they call it a "B♭" instrument when it is truly an A♭ instrument in terms of orchestral nomenclature.

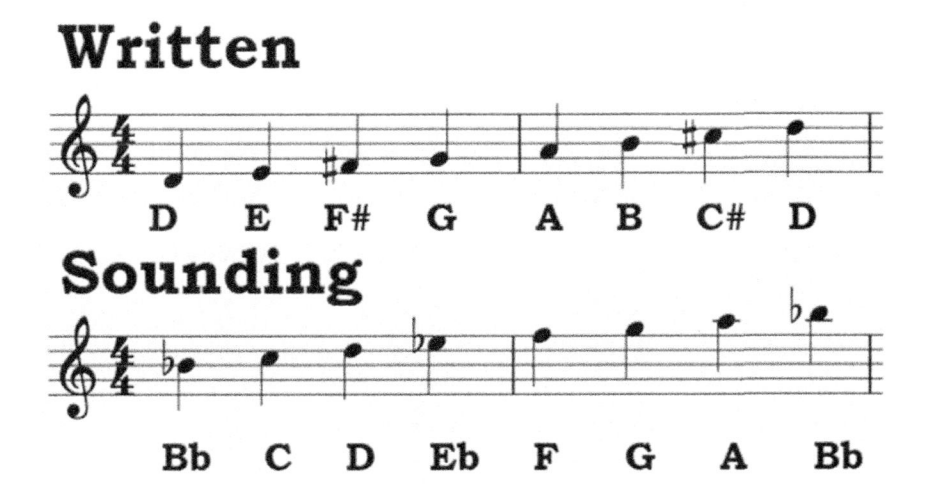

Written

D E F# G A B C# D

Sounding

B♭ C D E♭ F G A B♭

Written

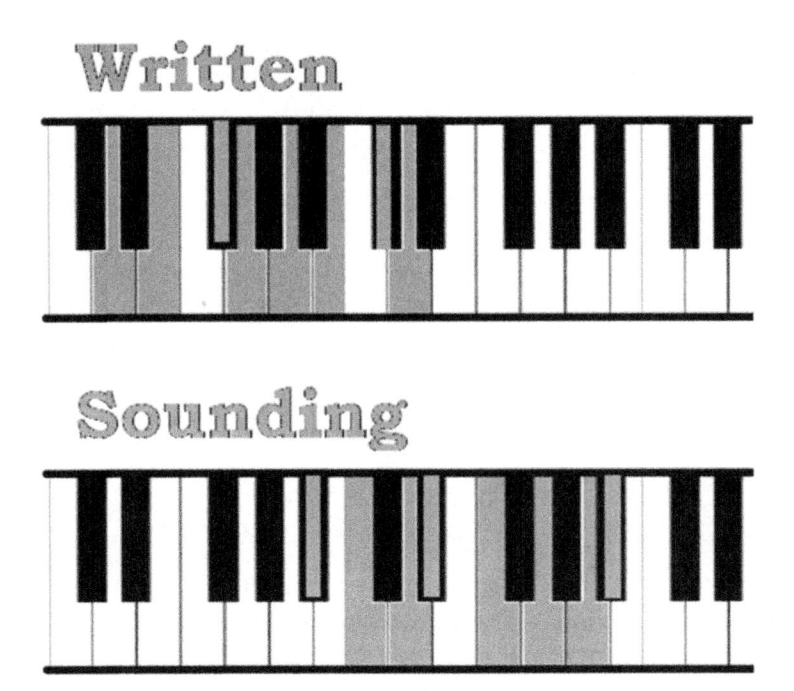

Sounding

What all of this means is that you cannot play in an ensemble with other players using the same sheet music. Every note on sheet music for the fife will be different by the same degree. For the same reason, a trumpeter could not play with a piano using the same sheet music. Trumpet transposes, but piano does not. If you are hoping to jam with friends, be sure to ask them what key they are in and what key that makes you for an instrument that sounds an A^b at a written C, or a B^b for a D, which is the same interval.

Now that we've discussed this, it's important to note that all the sheet music in this book is transposed for the fife. That means you will read a D, but you will hear a B^b. So, to start, let's take a look at getting a tuned note from your fife. This sound file will play a B♭. But it won't be written as a B♭, it will be written as D. To avoid confusion, from here on in the book, we will address every note as the transposed note. That means this sound file will play a "D", but we know it really isn't a D, right?

The last major note is that fifes are being contemporized and there are various kinds now. It's important to know what key your fife is playing in and if that key relates to C or to D, like traditional fifes. We'll test it with the next sound file.

Cover all the finger holes and play a single note to see if you are in tune. This note you're playing is a D (written, not sounding).

> **Listening Sound File #1**
> Listen to a written D note on the fife.
> (This note is written as D, but is sounding as a real B♭ note.

https://soundcloud.com/jason_randall/sets/how-to-play-the-fife?utm_source=clipboard&utm_medium=text&utm_campaign=social_sharing

Practice rolling in and out to get your pitch as close as possible. If, however, your note is way off, it means your fife is not your fault. The fife might not be in a traditional key.

If your fife is in a different key, there is a possibility the written D note is sounding a C or even an actual sounding, non-transposed D note. In those cases, use the book's audio files to get the idea of relative pitch, but don't play along with them, as the notes will be different in every audio sample of the book. This book's audio is made for a standardly tuned fife.

Taking Care of the Fife

Basic care for the fife is dependent on the material it's made of. Some fifes will be metal, which will require little upkeep aside from hygienic cleaning, polishing, and rust prevention.

Wooden fifes require more attention. These will usually be constructed from granadilla, cocobolo, boxwood, or ebony. They are prone to crack or chip if not cared for properly. During the first two months, new fifes should be oiled once or twice a week. After that, during the next eight months, oil these wooden fifes once a month, and finally two or three times annually for the rest of its life.

Fifers tend to clean their instrument after each use, drying it by swabbing it with a cloth both inside and out. Old time fifers would let vegetable oil sit in their fifes overnight, which is fine but not always necessary.

Taking Breaks

As mentioned, playing the fife will have your body working in ways you aren't familiar with, especially if you're holding the instrument correctly and maintaining good posture. Fifers shouldn't push themselves to do too much in large doses. Take breaks if you start to get sore, otherwise you might be out of commission for a couple days after when your neck muscles and shoulders are aching.

The main areas that will strain are your wrists, shoulders, and neck. Before picking up the fife, wiggle your wrists, shake your hands, and roll your shoulders. This will warm up the muscles before they sustain awkward positions when playing. Do this after playing, too, so the blood flows and keeps the muscles in check.

Chapter 3
Understanding Music Notes and Rhythm

Topics Covered:

- Beginner sight-reading

- The musical staff and its notes

- Rhythmic values of notes

- Time signature

- Key signatures

Musicians have a specific, internationally standardized language to share their compositions. It's this language that allows professional performers to play a piece they've never heard before with a simple transcription on paper. The ability to read music is called sight-reading, and it can take years to master. However, being comfortable with deciphering sheet music is important and, with practice, it will become more natural. We can hear compositions written before audio recording technology was available thanks to these standards for writing music.

The Musical Staff

All music is written on transcripts with five horizontal lines. This is called the musical staff. Each line on the staff is a note. And each space on the staff is a note. Because of the human ear's ability to hear frequencies from 20hz to 20,000hz, these five lines are not sufficient to show every note. Therefore, musicians use notations known as clefs to distinguish the octave.

Treble Clef | **Bass Clef** | **Alto Clef**

The first is the treble clef, followed by the alto clef, and finally the bass clef. There are other clefs, but these are the most often used. As a fifer, you'll be getting to know the treble clef. Notes on the treble clef are easiest remembered by knowing the notes in the four spaces. On the way up, they spell "FACE". This is a good pneumonic to navigate the treble staff.

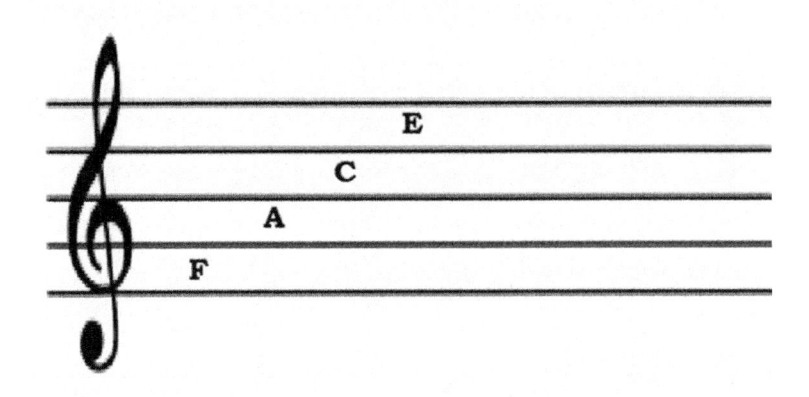

The notes travel up in alphabetical order, space to line to space to line, etc. So, before the F on the first space, the note E is on the line. The line between the space for F and the space for A is the G note, because it simply goes in order.

The important thing to remember is that all notes go from A alphabetically to G, then they return to A, but this new A is an octave higher. Then it continues in the same way.

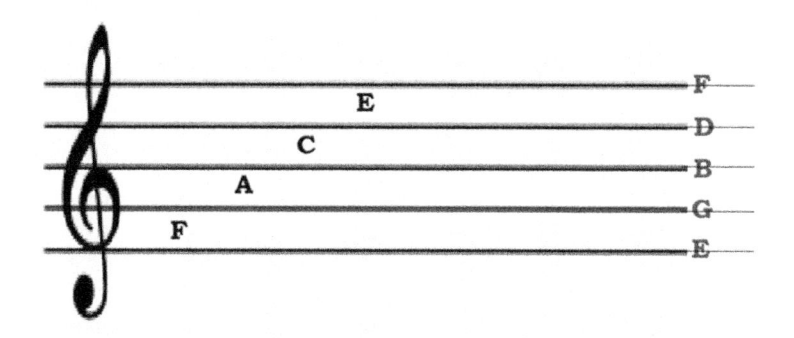

These are always the notes on the treble staff. There are times when the note is adjusted slightly with accidentals. Accidentals are sharps and flats. A sharp note is marked with a "#", and a flat note is marked with a "b". So, a C sharp is written C#. A B flat is written Bb. C# still resides on the C space, but it is a different note. Bb still resides on the B line, but it is a different note.

Bb C#

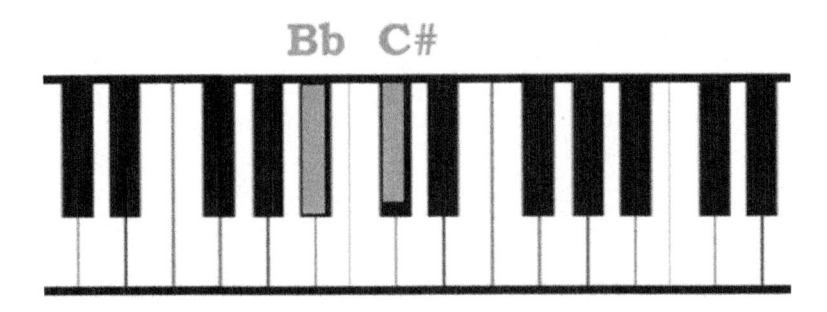

Sometimes you will see a natural sign in front of a note. This means that it was changed to a sharp or a flat, but now we want to hear the normal note. In other words, if the player is expecting to play a C# but they should actually just play C, they'll see it labeled as ♮ to show it's natural. Of course, unlabeled lines and spaces are always the natural.

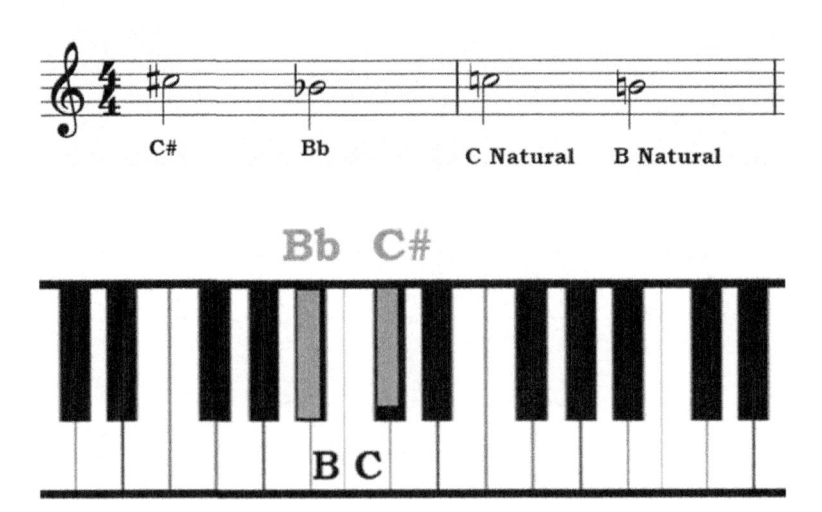

C#   Bb   C Natural   B Natural

Bb C#

B C

A piano is an easy way to see what notes are natural and what notes are sharps and flats. The white keys are all natural notes, while the black keys are both a sharp or a flat, depending on context. Notice that an A# is exactly the same key on the piano as a B♭. The reasons why a black note can be either a sharp or a flat is only due to the context of the key signature the song is in. The traditional fife plays only sharp notes and never has to worry about calling them flat notes.

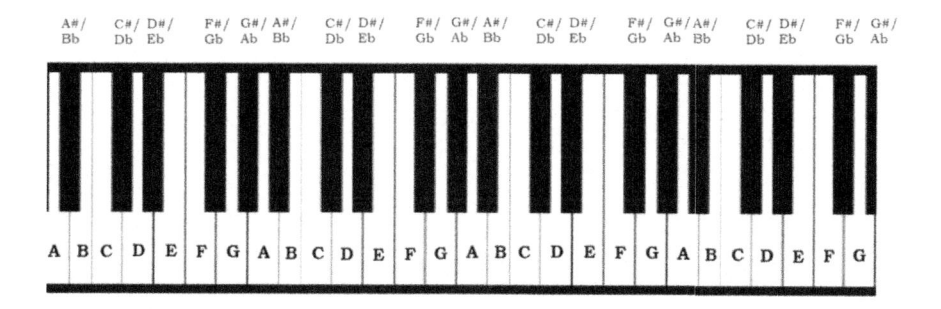

Notes can get higher and lower than what we see on the treble staff. For higher notes, musicians write more lines, still using the spaces, as well. A high C note will be on two lines above the normal staff. Count the lines and spaces as you know them, following them alphabetically up to C. Remember to go from G to A.

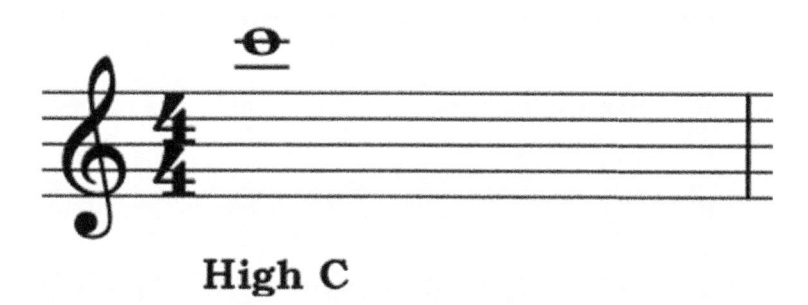

High C

Lower notes are done in the very same way, just by adding short reference lines below the staff. Middle C is the first line below the staff. Additionally, if we go one space downward and down again to the next line, we'll come to the A an octave below concert A.

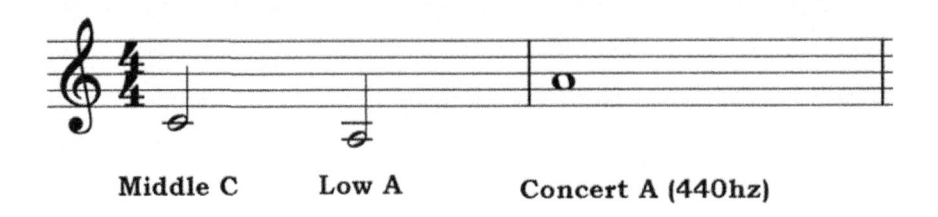

Middle C   **Low A**   **Concert A (440hz)**

Rhythmic Values of Notes

To read music, a player must understand the rhythmic value of notes. Notes are based on divisions of time. It starts with a whole note, then we divide by two to get the half note. The half note is then divided by two again to get a quarter note. A quarter note then is divided by two again to get an eighth note and so on to the sixteenth note, the thirty-second note, and the sixty-fourth note. For each subdivision after the eighth note, notice that we add a "flag" to the note stem. The sixteenth note has two flags, and the thirty-second note has three flags. Anything beyond a sixteenth note is rare, but in modern composition higher divisions are becoming more common.

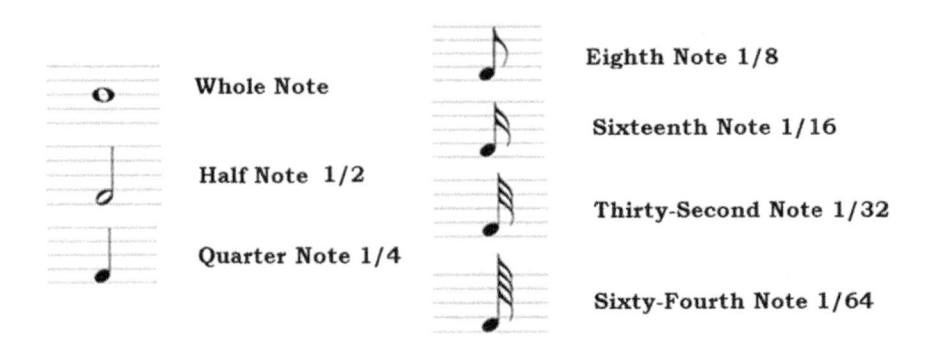

Whole Note

Half Note 1/2

Quarter Note 1/4

Eighth Note 1/8

Sixteenth Note 1/16

Thirty-Second Note 1/32

Sixty-Fourth Note 1/64

Understanding Music Notes and Rhythm

When there are two or more notes that are an eighth or sixteenth, the flags can connect. Two eighths will connect their bar to look like a bar. This is done to make music easier to count. Another thing to be aware of is that the note stems can go up or down, depending on their location. If they are higher on the staff, the stem will usually be going down, and if they are on the lower part of the staff, the stem will be going up.

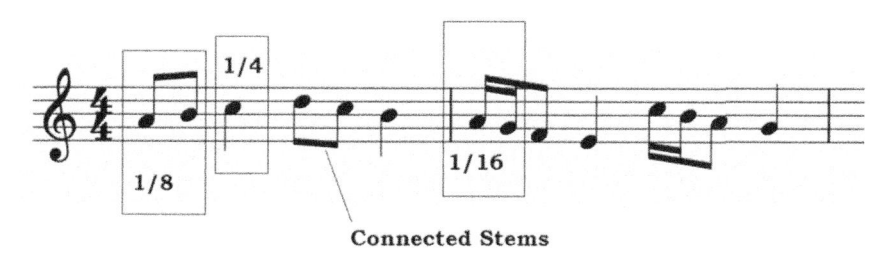

Connected Stems

A whole note gets a whole beat, while a half note gets half a beat. In other words, two half notes would fit into the time it takes to play one whole note. The time between each of these half notes is exactly the same. To illustrate the rhythm of a whole note and half note, listen to the audio file and tap along. The bass drum will play the whole note while the snare will play the half note. Play the whole notes with your right hand and the half notes with your left, which is double the speed.

> **Listening Sound File #2**
> Listen to the rhythm and tap along.

https://soundcloud.com/jason_randall/sets/how-to-play-the-fife?utm_source=clipboard&utm_medium=text&utm_campaign=social_sharing

The rhythm can be written another way, too. Instead of whole notes and half notes, we can use quarter notes and eighth notes. This will get us the same exact sound, because an eighth note is half the length of a quarter note. The only difference is the *tempo*.

Tempo is the speed of a song. Every song has a tempo, and some change tempos throughout. Tempos are usually written in relation to the quarter note, and they are measured in beats per minute.

♩ = 120

A very common tempo is 120. This is easy to find, because it means that a quarter note happens 120 times in a minute. 120 beats per minute. This also means a half note happens 60 times a minute, so a half note happens every second on the second.

Conductors can use watches to find their tempo if it's easily subdividing a minute like 120BPM.

Next, look at sixteenth notes played over quarter notes. It will take four sixteenth notes to equal one quarter note. This tempo will be at 60.

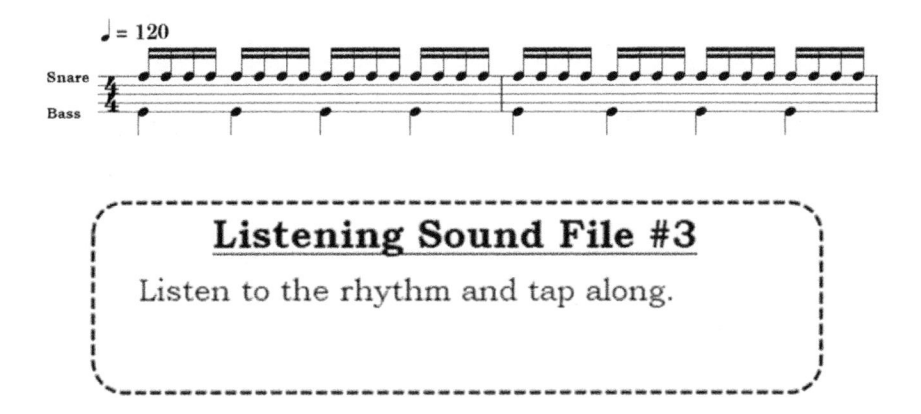

> **Listening Sound File #3**
> Listen to the rhythm and tap along.

https://soundcloud.com/jason_randall/sets/how-to-play-the-fife?utm_source=clipboard&utm_medium=text&utm_campaign=social_sharing

Rhythm isn't always so easy. Sometimes you will have multiple subdivisions in a song. Just remember that it is based on playing doubly fast for each division. This means each subdivision is named for how much more quickly it is played in relation to a whole note. A sixteenth happens sixteen times as fast as a whole note. Take a look at the next rhythm. This will have both eighths and sixteenths playing over a quarter note. The click will show you where the whole note is.

[Musical notation: ♩ = 120, Snare/Bass/Click pattern in 4/4]

> **Listening Sound File #4**
>
> Listen to the rhythm and tap along.

https://soundcloud.com/jason_randall/sets/how-to-play-the-fife?utm_source=clipboard&utm_medium=text&utm_campaign=social_sharing

Practice tapping different rhythms. Try these, then try writing your own to tap.

[Musical notation: ♩ = 120, 4/4 rhythm exercises]

> **Listening Sound File #5**
>
> Listen to the rhythm and tap along.

https://soundcloud.com/jason_randall/sets/how-to-play-the-fife?utm_source=clipboard&utm_medium=text&utm_campaign=social_sharing

Understanding Music Notes and Rhythm

♩ = 120

[musical notation in 4/4 time]

```
┌─────────────────────────────────────┐
│     Listening Sound File #6         │
│   Listen to the rhythm and tap along. │
└─────────────────────────────────────┘
```

https://soundcloud.com/jason_randall/sets/how-to-play-the-fife?utm_source=clipboard&utm_medium=text&utm_campaign=social_sharing

♩ = 120

[musical notation in 4/4 time]

```
┌─────────────────────────────────────┐
│     Listening Sound File #7         │
│   Listen to the rhythm and tap along. │
└─────────────────────────────────────┘
```

https://soundcloud.com/jason_randall/sets/how-to-play-the-fife?utm_source=clipboard&utm_medium=text&utm_campaign=social_sharing

Note values show us when and how long we are supposed to play each note. A whole note for a fife means that the note is held for the entire duration of that note. However, sometimes players are not supposed to play for a certain amount of time. For this, we need to understand rests.

Rests

Notes tell us when to play, rests tell us when not to play. Rests have the same way of being divided by two. There is a whole rest, a half rest, and subsequent further subdivisions like the quarter, eighth, sixteenth, and so on. The diagram shows how we write rests. To differentiate between a whole rest and half rest, remember this pneumonic: A whole gentleman takes his hat off, and half a gentleman leaves his hat on. The whole rest is on the upper line, resembling a removed hat, while the half rest is on the line, like a worn hat.

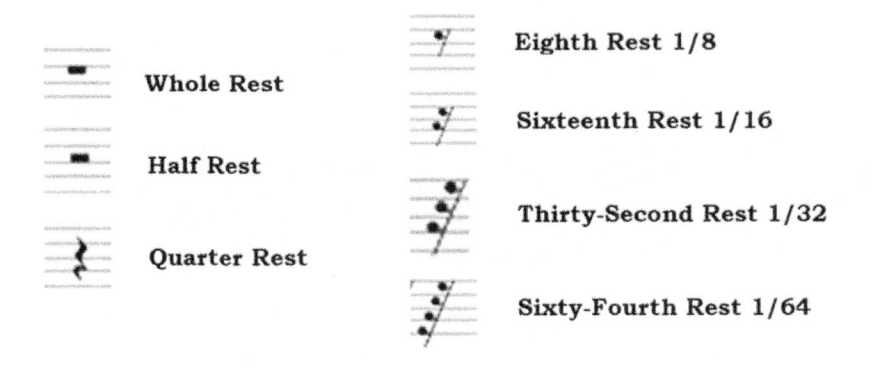

Whole Rest

Half Rest

Quarter Rest

Eighth Rest 1/8

Sixteenth Rest 1/16

Thirty-Second Rest 1/32

Sixty-Fourth Rest 1/64

With rhythm, it would be the same if we saw a half note and a half rest or just one whole note. Two halves make a whole. The reason it matters, though, is because when we play the fife, we will only sound a note for the duration of a half note. Don't worry about playing the fife yet, but listen to the way the written notes will be played with rests.

Understanding Music Notes and Rhythm

[Musical notation: Fife and Drums, ♩ = 120, 4/4 time]

> **Listening Sound File #8**
> Listen to the rhythm and tap along.

https://soundcloud.com/jason_randall/sets/how-to-play-the-fife?utm_source=clipboard&utm_medium=text&utm_campaign=social_sharing

Practice understanding these rest and note relationships with one more audio file.

[Musical notation: Fife and Snare, ♩ = 120, 4/4 time]

> **Listening Sound File #9**
> Listen to the rhythm and tap along.

https://soundcloud.com/jason_randall/sets/how-to-play-the-fife?utm_source=clipboard&utm_medium=text&utm_campaign=social_sharing

Dotted Notes

Rhythm can become quite complicated, especially in modern composition. However, the furthest fife music will take rhythm is with dotted notes. Dotted notes are an abbreviated way of writing a note plus one of the same note's next subdivisions. In other words, a dotted quarter note would be the same as a quarter note plus an eighth note. The same is true for every subdivision.

Dotted notes can get more complicated by being double-dotted. Double-dotted notes are not too common, but they mean that the note adds the length of the next subdivision as well as the length of the next subdivision from this subdivision. In other words, a double-dotted quarter note would be a quarter plus an eighth plus a sixteenth.

$$\note{half..} = \note{half} + \note{quarter} + \note{eighth}$$

$$\note{quarter..} = \note{quarter} + \note{eighth} + \note{sixteenth}$$

$$\note{eighth..} = \note{eighth} + \note{sixteenth} + \note{thirty-second}$$

$$\note{sixteenth..} = \note{sixteenth} + \note{thirty-second} + \note{sixty-fourth}$$

These are rare, and as you begin to learn the fife, you shouldn't have to worry about any double-dotted notes. You will see dotted notes, though, so be on your guard for them. Practice tapping along with some dotted notes.

♩ = 120

***

> **Listening Sound File #10**
> Listen to the rhythm and tap along.

https://soundcloud.com/jason_randall/sets/how-to-play-the-fife?utm_source=clipboard&utm_medium=text&utm_campaign=social_sharing

Time Signature

When looking at a new piece of music, players need to know how to count it out. The time signature is the signifier of what type of "count" a song has behind it. Dancers use this time signature in the same way. A time signature will have one number over another number. Unless it changes, it will only appear at the beginning of the staff. The only time you will see a different format for a time signature is if you see semi-circle "C". This means it is in common time, which another way of saying a time signature of 4/4.

$$\frac{2}{4} \quad \frac{3}{4} \quad \frac{4}{4} \quad \frac{3}{2}$$

Music is divided by measures. A measure is basically like a sentence in the music. The time signature tells the player how many notes go in one measure. The top numbers and the bottom numbers mean different things. The top number of a time signature tells you how many notes are in the measure, while the bottom number tells you what kind of note goes in the bottom. In other words, a 3/4 time signature has three quarter notes in one measure. A 4/4 time signature has four quarter notes in one measure. And something odd like a 10/16 time signature has ten sixteenth notes in one measure. Fife music will tend to be in 4/4 (common time) or 3/4, so you won't have to worry about these stranger time signatures.

Understanding Music Notes and Rhythm

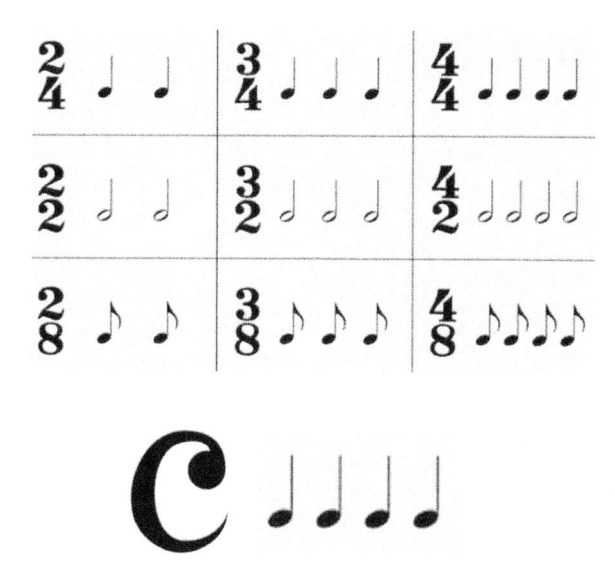

$\frac{2}{4}$ ♩ ♩	$\frac{3}{4}$ ♩ ♩ ♩	$\frac{4}{4}$ ♩ ♩ ♩ ♩
$\frac{2}{2}$ ♩ ♩	$\frac{3}{2}$ ♩ ♩ ♩	$\frac{4}{2}$ ♩ ♩ ♩ ♩
$\frac{2}{8}$ ♪ ♪	$\frac{3}{8}$ ♪ ♪ ♪	$\frac{4}{8}$ ♪ ♪ ♪ ♪

C ♩ ♩ ♩ ♩

Just because a time is 4/4 doesn't mean you'll only see four quarter notes. In the time of four quarter notes, you can see any subdivision, depending on the rhythm of the song. For instance, one measure of a 4/4 song might have two eighths and three quarters, which is the same amount of time as four quarter notes.

Practice writing some rhythms in 4/4 and 3/4. See if you can also tap along to whatever you write. Try to challenge yourself by writing trickier rhythms.

Counting

As you play the fife, it's important to keep a steady tempo. A metronome is an excellent tool to use while practicing. It helps keep the tempo consistent and will help you count out rhythm.

Musicians tend to count music with integers on the notes in the time signature. A 4/4 would be counted 1, 2, 3, 4 on the quarter notes. To count eighths, musicians say, "1, and, 2, and, 3, and, 4, and..." Every "and" is the eighth that is off-beat. The numbers are on-beat. To count sixteenths, musicians count, "1-ee-and-uh, 2-ee-and-uh, 3-ee-and-uh, 4-ee-and-uh..." Depending on where the notes land, you'll play them or you'll wait to play them. This can take a lot of practice. Try tapping some rhythms and counting out loud. You can use some of the previous sheet music as practice. And get in the habit of doing this before learning any new song.

Key Signatures

Behind the time signatures, at the beginning of the staff, you might see key signatures. A key is the scale the song is played in. Most tonal music plays in a major or minor scale, which include the exact same pattern just moved and a change in starting point. C major has the exact same set of notes as A *minor*, they are just phrased differently. D major, the most common key signature for fife, has the same intervals as any major scale, it is just moved to align with D as its first note. This can be most easily seen on a piano.

C Major Scale

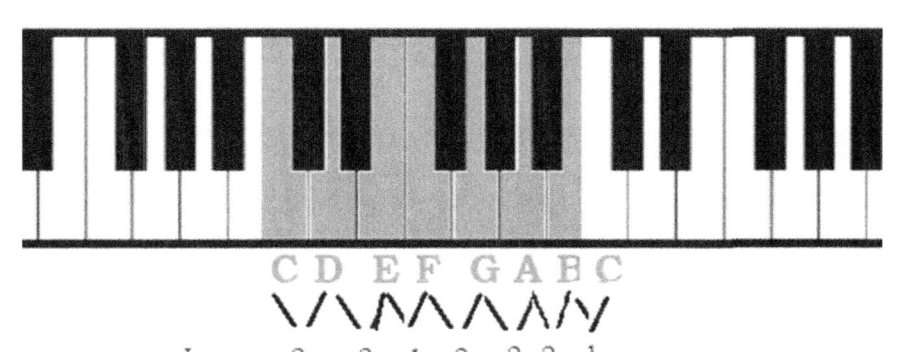

C D E F G A B C
\/\/\ /\/\ /\ /\ /\/
Jump: 2 2 1 2 2 2 1

D Major Scale

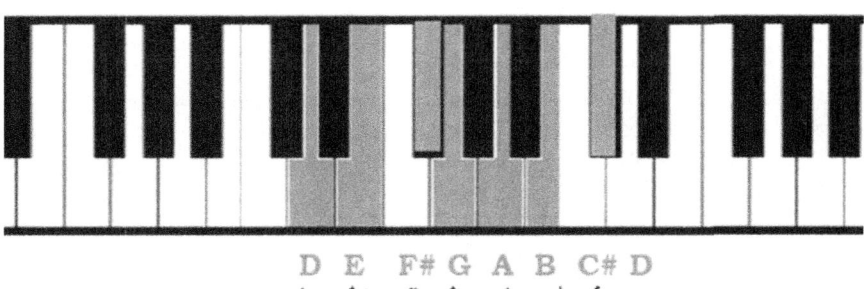

D E F# G A B C# D
\/\/\ /\/\ /\ /\ /\/
Jump: 2 2 1 2 2 2 1

D major has two sharps. The sharps of D major are F# and C#. This means that the notes in D major are D, E, F#, G, A, B, and C#. Key signatures only show the unnatural notes, meaning the sharps or flats.

D Major Key Signature
(Marking for the D Major Scale)

Other common key signatures for the fife are G major and A major. These have the same pattern of skipping notes, but starting on their beginning note, G or A.

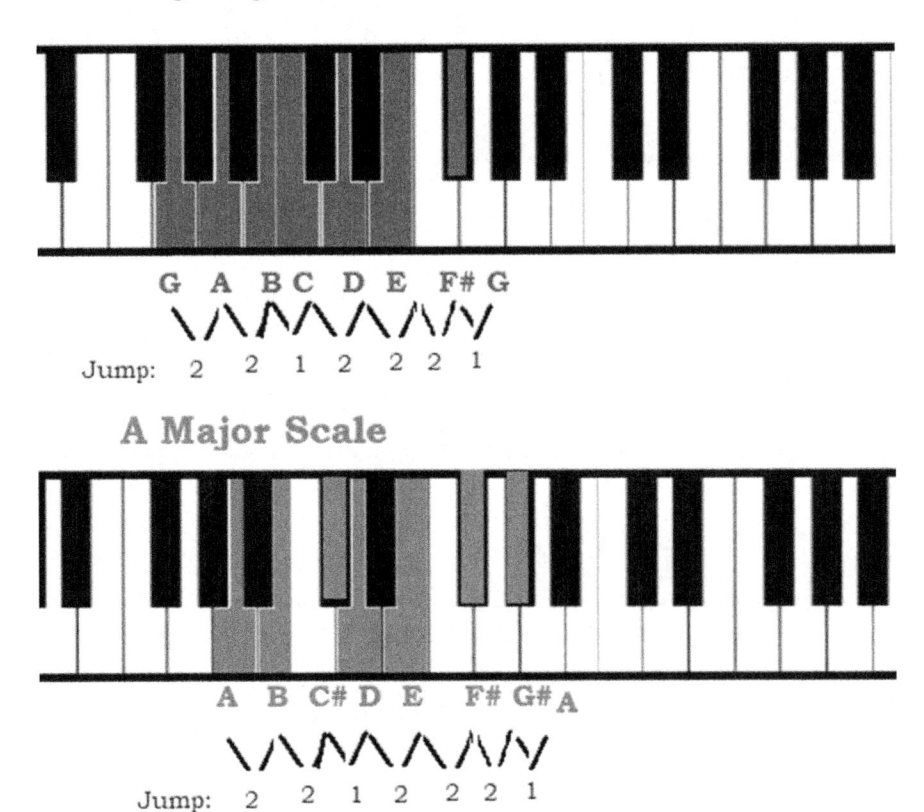

G A B C D E F# G
\ /\ /\ /\ /\ /\ /\ /
Jump: 2 2 1 2 2 2 1

A Major Scale

A B C# D E F# G# A
\ /\ /\ /\ /\ /\ /\ /
Jump: 2 2 1 2 2 2 1

The key signatures have different amounts of sharps, with G major having one sharp (F#) and A major having three sharps (F#, C#, and G#).

G Major Key Signature   **A Major Key Signature**

Transposition Revisited

The idea behind transposition gets even more confusing with the fife. We know that a written D means a sounding actual note of B♭. But that is not all. The fife is also written an octave lower than it sounds. This means that the sounding B♭ is up an octave from the B♭ above the written D. This is not too important unless you're going to play with other note-playing musicians.

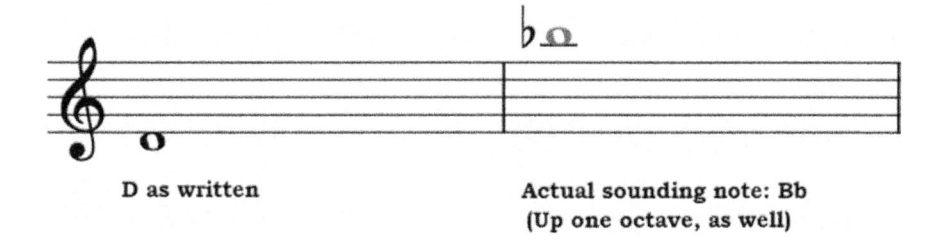

D as written   **Actual sounding note: Bb**
                     (Up one octave, as well)

This is the last time transposition will be mentioned. For the rest of the book, as you learn to play the fife, the notes will be called what they are as written.

Chapter 4
How to Play Notes on the Fife

Topics Covered:

- Getting your first note

- Range

- Fingering for usual notes

- D major scale

- Breathing considerations and practices

Getting your first notes out of the fife will be the most difficult hurtle. This has most to do with embouchure, posture, and fife position. If you pay attention to these three main things, you'll manage to get a sound out of it. For a quick review on these three main considerations, revisit Chapter 2 on how to hold the fife and embouchure.

Getting Your First Note

Firstly, focus on getting a D out of the fife. Pick up the fife as described in Chapter 2. Be sure to stand up. Don't sit down. Square your shoulders with your hips and stand steady. Start by covering all the holes. The most common D note is achieved by lifting your index finger on your left hand so every hole is covered except the first. Don't change your finger position until you get this first note. Be sure the index finger is fully removed from the hole and not in the way at all, while all the other holes are fully covered with no air escaping from your other fingers' placement.

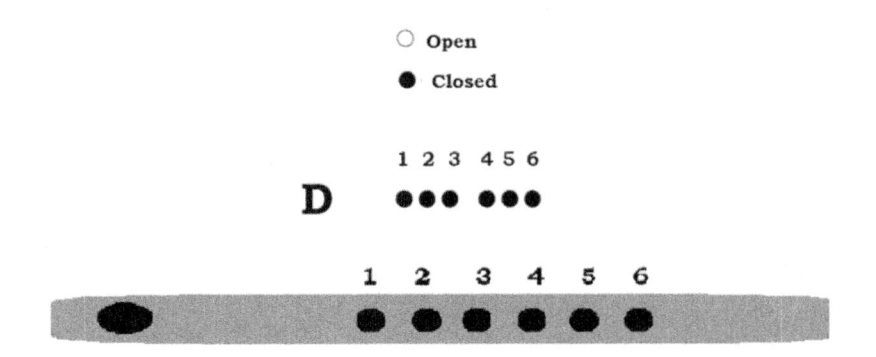

○ Open
● Closed

```
      1 2 3  4 5 6
  D   ●●●  ●●●
```

Correct embouchure won't quickly tire your lips, so remember to keep them tight but not strained. It should feel something like a strange smile. If you purse your lips too much, you won't get a sound. Try to imagine a person with tight lips trying to fight the urge to smile and it will allow the opening between your lips just barely able to blow out.

If it's still too difficult to get the right embouchure, start by relaxing your lips. Place the fife at the direct center of your bottom lip. Then, use the fife to push your relaxed bottom lip upwards to cover your top lip. From here, push air to the front of your cheeks like a hamster, pushing the air out and nearly downward. This will create a very small gap where air escapes. Another practice is to act like a rabbit, lifting the muscles of your upper lip near the nostril. This way of lifting your top lip is what controls the flow of air. The air, itself, should be coming from the front of your nearly closed mouth.

Fifers instinctively roll the fife so the blowhole lines up better. Roll in toward your lips or slightly away. Most fifers roll in, which slightly flattens the pitch. Rolling out slightly sharpens the pitch.

The note should sound pure without any scratchiness. To fix scratchy, impure tones, try rolling in and out or adjusting your lip position.

Range

The fife is capable of making sound across three octaves. The lowest octave of its range is seldom used. The middle octave is what is used most often. The highest octave is more difficult to achieve. It requires faster speed of air into the fife.

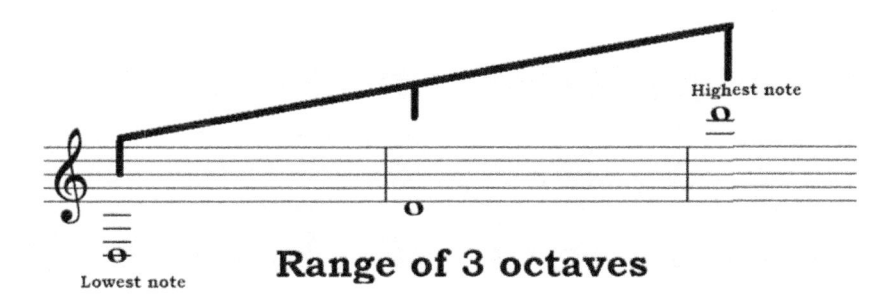

Range of 3 octaves

Fingering for Notes

The fife works by allowing air to be tunneled to the right frequency, which creates a specific note. The finger holes allow air at certain key locations to escape, changing the frequency that the instrument makes. The pattern behind the science of it isn't intuitive, so it is best to remember the fingering for each note. However, because it is an instrument based on the frequency of air, higher notes can be achieved with faster traveling air. So, the faster air leaves the mouth, the more frequency the air inside the fife is experiencing, which can change to note. You'll see the same fingering pattern for two different notes is the same sometimes. This means that when blowing with more pressure and creating faster air flow, you'll achieve the higher of the two notes, whichever they might be. The good thing is that these two notes are all that will be achieved with the fingering pattern, so you'll only have to distinguish between the higher and the lower to know how hard to push the air out.

The most common scale played on the fife is the D major scale. You'll see these notes the most. Take a look at the chart below and how to play each note. Focus on the middle octave first and try to get each note. Then, move on to the lower octave.

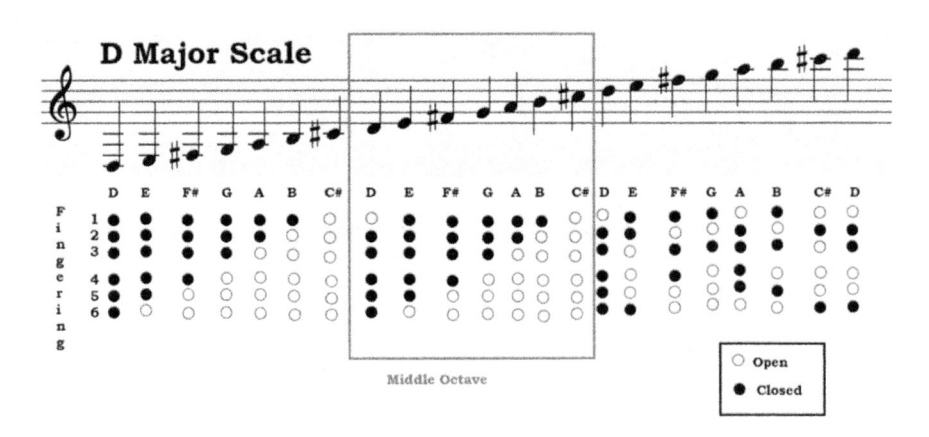

Changing High and Low Notes

Next, focus on the low E and middle E. These have the same fingering. See if you can achieve each note with intention. To get the higher of the two, breathe out with a slightly different shaped embouchure. This is the easiest way to change the frequency of airflow. A more downward burst of air will get the lower notes. A more upward-blown air burst will get the higher notes. Practice first by using your jaw to go back. This makes your upper lip further out than your bottom lip, creating downward airflow. As you push your jaw forward, the bottom lip will roll out and eventually become further forward than your upper lip. The shape of your lips and the way you use your upper lip muscles near your nostril will slightly change as you try to achieve either downward or upward airflow. Practice getting two notes from one fingering pattern.

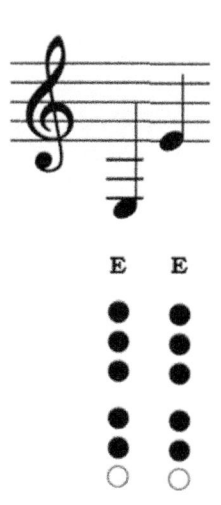

An important thing to note is that you might be doing the higher note or the lower note. Try to adjust both ways until you get a low E and a high E. This is the same note, just an octave higher. You'll hear the difference, but the character of the note will be the same.

Beginning fifers will be able to play the first two octaves of the D major scale with ease. Practice making your own melodies with these notes. Don't worry about rhythm at first, just practice changing between the notes. Be aware of what notes you're playing and say them in your head as you play them. Try to do this without looking at the fingering chart eventually. Sheet music will not always have the fingering pattern below each note, but as a fifer it will become second-nature knowing how to sound each note without a chart.

Chapter 5
Playing Your First Songs

Topics Covered:

- Warm-ups

- Playing D, G, and A scales

- Reading songs

- Easy beginner songs

Once you're able to produce sound from the fife, learning songs will be a more easily achievable next step. Most songs for the fife feature a solo melody line accompanied by a drum line without any other harmonization. Being involved in marching bands means it is important to keep tempo as a fifer.

The Metronome

Keeping time is integral. While you don't always need to be perfectly at tempo, any major deviation will sound odd and change the feeling of any song. There are two ways to make sure you are keeping time. One way is to get a metronome. You can listen to the beeps as you play and set any tempo or time signature on these time-keeping devices. There are also free apps that emulate metronomes, so it doesn't need to be another expenditure.

Another way to make sure you're in time is the practice of marching in place. The fife was used as a marching instrument, and marching bands know how to march at the right tempo. To march appropriately, make sure you have the same step at the same note value. Most often, musicians march with their right foot landing on the 1 and the 3 of each bar in a 4/4 time signature. This means their left foot is landing on the 2 and 4 of a 4/4 bar. If the time is 3/4, the march will obviously be a bit different as the numbers aren't easily divisible. The right foot may land on 1 and 3, then on 2 of the subsequent bar. If the tempo of the song is slow enough, marchers can make each step land on every quarter value in a 4/4, meaning it lands at 1, 2, 3, and 4. At this speed, the left foot will be landing on the eighth note value between each right foot step. In counting, these left steps would be on the "and".

Find whatever march is most comfortable for you. The main thing is to be consistent so that you are keeping the same tempo. Don't slow your march to change the duration of notes, or it will change the song. This practice isn't used solely for marching bands. Many music teachers for violin have their students march in time if their rhythm is not satisfactory. However, if marching seems silly or obscures your breath, you can change the march to a simple foot tap. Tapping your foot on the 1, 2, 3, 4 works well, but it may give way to more erroneous deviation in tempo. A steady march is hard to deviate from.

Warm-Ups and Scales

Before playing any songs, it's a good idea to play simple long notes in time. Start with four consecutive notes as whole notes. Keep tempo as you change each note at each bar.

Playing Your First Songs

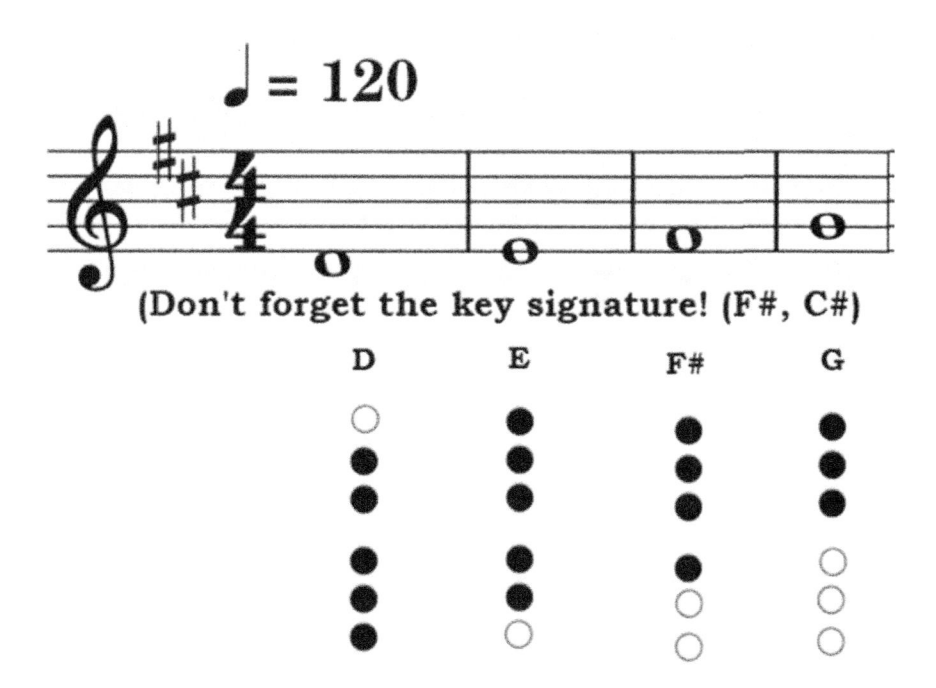

♩ = 120

(Don't forget the key signature! (F#, C#)

D   E   F#   G

Listening Sound File #11
Practice playing four whole notes in rhythm.

https://soundcloud.com/jason_randall/sets/how-to-play-the-fife?utm_source=clipboard&utm_medium=text&utm_campaign=social_sharing

Next, practice playing every note of the D major scale in time.

How To Play The Fife

(Don't forget the key signature! (F#, C#)

> **Listening Sound File #12**
> Practice playing a D major scale in whole notes.

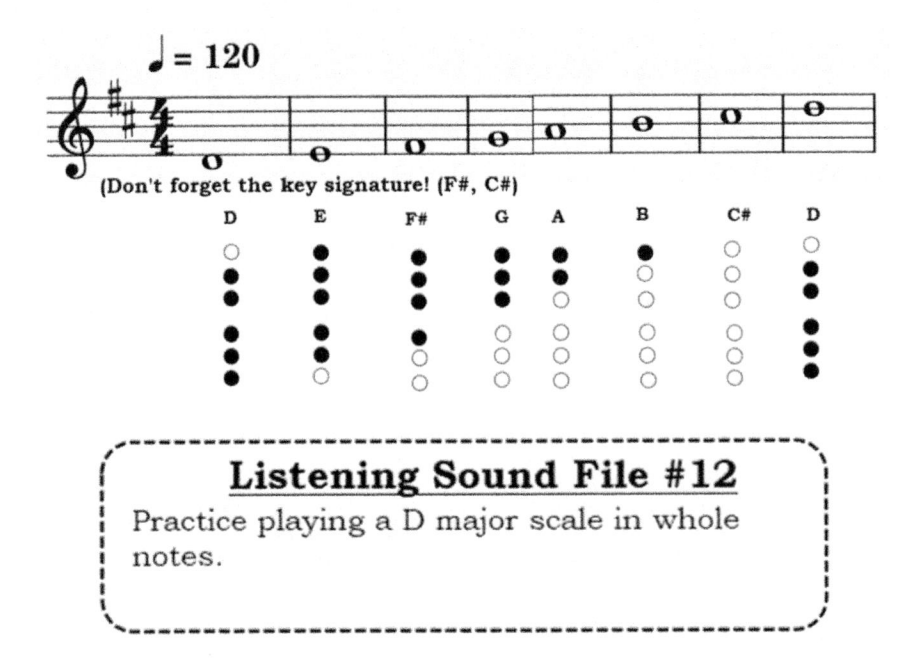

https://soundcloud.com/jason_randall/sets/how-to-play-the-fife?utm_source=clipboard&utm_medium=text&utm_campaign=social_sharing

The D major scale is one of three main scales for the fife. You may also need to play in G major or A major. Luckily, these scales are similar. G major has an F#, while D major has F# and C# notes. Finally, A major has three sharps, which are F#, C#, and G#. Practice playing each in time.

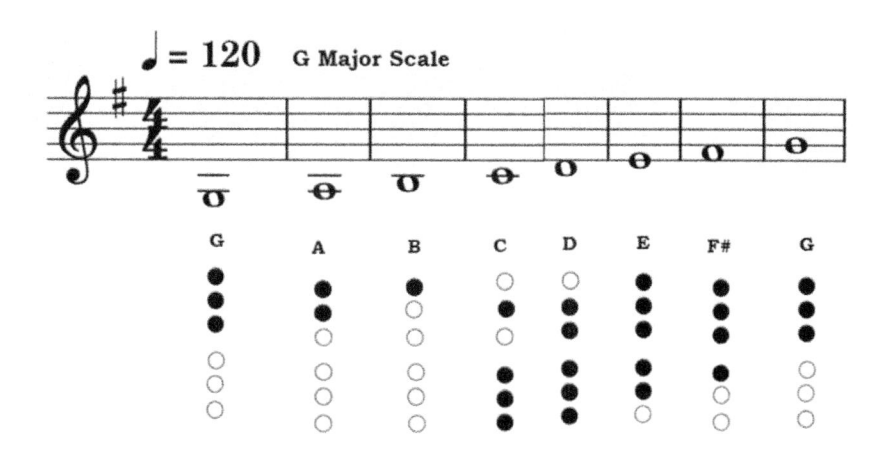

Playing Your First Songs

♩ = 120 G Major Scale

Listening Sound File #13

Practice a G major scale in whole notes.

https://soundcloud.com/jason_randall/sets/how-to-play-the-fife?utm_source=clipboard&utm_medium=text&utm_campaign=social_sharing

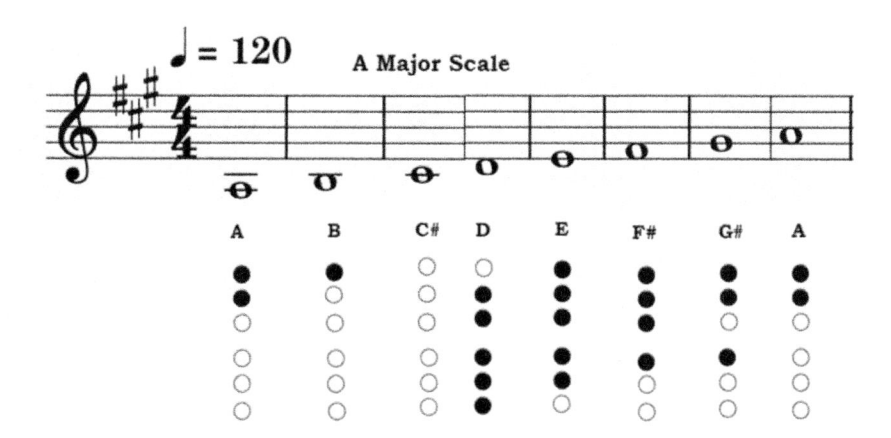

♩ = 120 A Major Scale

51

> ## Listening Sound File #14
> Practice an A major scale in whole notes.

https://soundcloud.com/jason_randall/sets/how-to-play-the-fife?utm_source=clipboard&utm_medium=text&utm_campaign=social_sharing

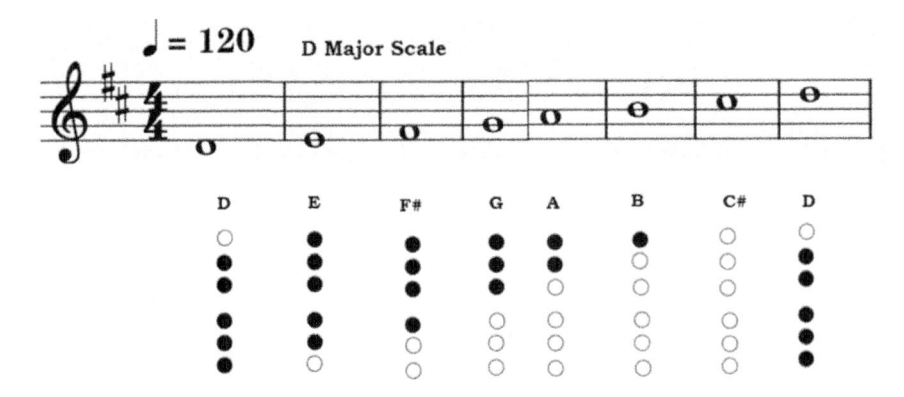

♩ = 120   D Major Scale

D	E	F#	G	A	B	C#	D
○	●	●	●	●	●	○	○
●	●	●	●	●	○	○	●
●	●	●	○	○	○	○	●
●	●	●	○	○	○	○	●
●	●	○	○	○	○	○	●
●	○	○	○	○	○	○	●

> ## Listening Sound File #12
> Practice playing a D major scale in whole notes.

https://soundcloud.com/jason_randall/sets/how-to-play-the-fife?utm_source=clipboard&utm_medium=text&utm_campaign=social_sharing

Free Jam

While professional musicians focus mostly on their musicality with precise tone and rhythm, there are ways to practice that can be more relaxed. Jamming is the practice of playing unwritten music, improvising notes as you feel and not as what somewhat else tells you to play. Any musician should be able to read and play compositions, but they should also know how to play what feels right to them. It is a balance of professionalism and creativity. While some prodigies are impeccable at playing even the most difficult compositions, some lack the ability to synthesize creatively within chords. Developing creativity is not only as important as perfecting structured techniques, it can also be much more fun and inspiring. The only caveat is to do this creative development with the intent to get more comfortable with the *proper* way of playing your instrument. Jamming can be counter-productive if you use improper techniques. So, while it is a more relaxed endeavor, the focus on technique should be at the forefront.

Jamming is best done with other musicians, but you can practice with some of these chord progressions. Again, if your fife is not traditionally tuned, it may be more difficult to find the key you need to jam in. As you play freely along, you'll notice not every note in the scale works as well as others over certain chords. This is good practice for your ear.

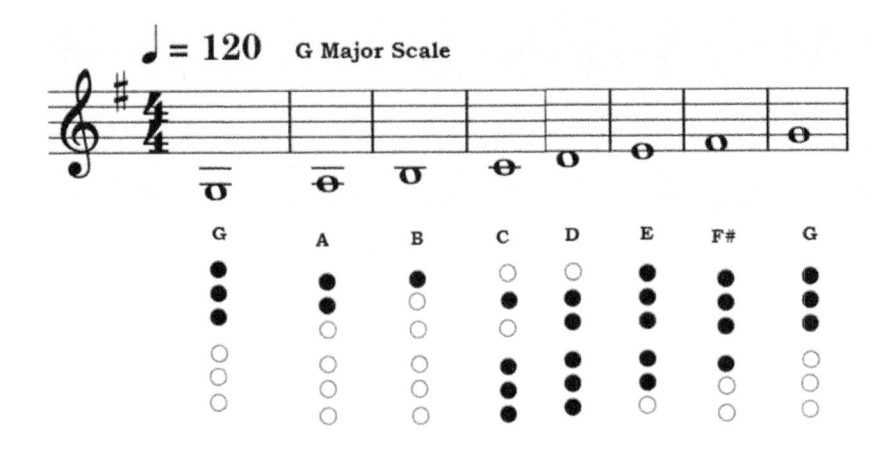

How To Play The Fife

♩ = 120 G Major Scale

Listening Sound File #15
Try playing any of the note in the scale to the song (if you have a traditionally tuned fife).

https://soundcloud.com/jason_randall/sets/how-to-play-the-fife?utm_source=clipboard&utm_medium=text&utm_campaign=social_sharing

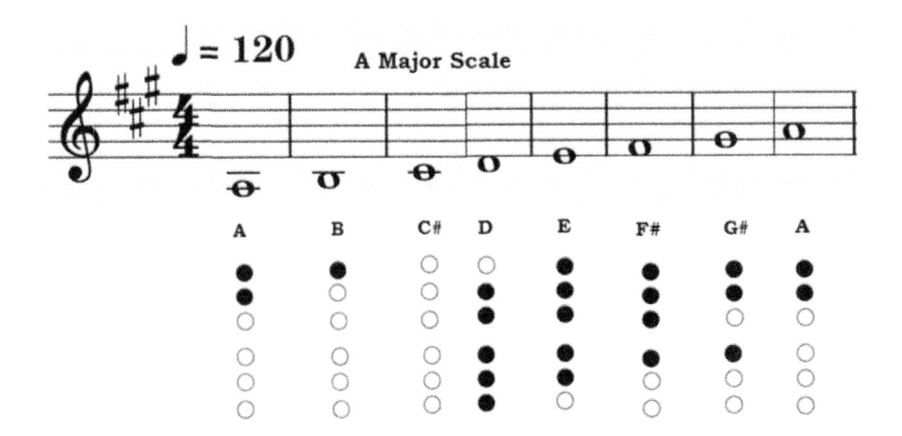

♩ = 120 A Major Scale

Playing Your First Songs

> **Listening Sound File #16**
> Try playing any of the note in the scale to the song (if you have a traditionally tuned fife).

https://soundcloud.com/jason_randall/sets/how-to-play-the-fife?utm_source=clipboard&utm_medium=text&utm_campaign=social_sharing

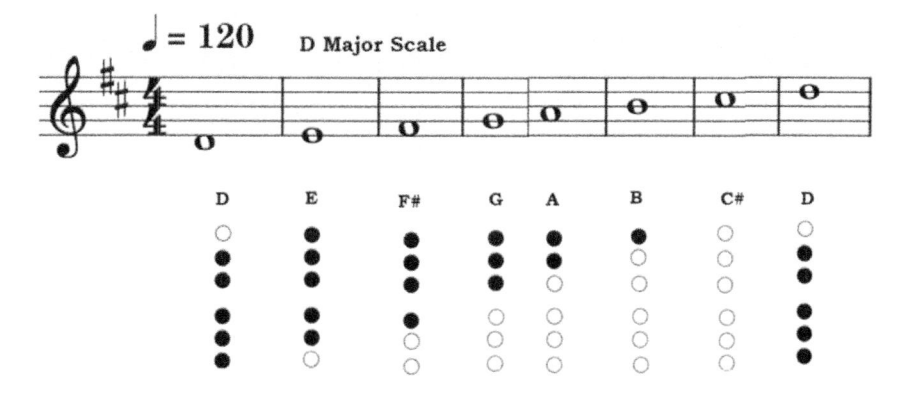

♩ = 120   D Major Scale

D E F# G A B C# D

> **Listening Sound File #17**
> Try playing any of the note in the scale to the song (if you have a traditionally tuned fife).

https://soundcloud.com/jason_randall/sets/how-to-play-the-fife?utm_source=clipboard&utm_medium=text&utm_campaign=social_sharing

Repeating Notation

In most sheet music, you will see notations for repetition. This notation is usually two horizontal dots at the beginning of a measure and also at the very end of a bar. It simply means that a passage within these two notations should be repeated once.

♩ = 120

Begin Repeat   End Repeat

Beginner Songs on the Fife

Jamming can be fun and less stressful. But an unrivaled way to get better at any instrument is to learn new songs. Composed songs show the player what musicians expect to do with their instrument. Simply playing what you want to play won't always illuminate new techniques.

Before starting any song, be sure to check some things out first. You want to be sure you're aware of the key signature (the scale), the time signature, and the tempo. Lastly, you want to get comfortable with the rhythm. If you don't have an audio reference, figure out the rhythm before you play any notes. Put the fife down and tap the rhythm of the notes with a hand as you march or tap your foot in time. Once you memorize or understand the rhythm, it will make playing the songs much easier.

While playing songs as a beginner, you might need to slow down the tempo. Make sure you keep a steady tempo, so if you slow the tempo down, keep that tempo for the whole song. It's best practice not to slow down the tempo unless you absolutely need to. Playing something slower doesn't mean you'll be as proficient at faster tempos. Instead of slowing down, just focus on sections that give you difficulty. Take any difficult portions of a song and practice them over and over again until you get good at them. Then you can practice segueing back into the song. Even if the section is only three quick notes, it'll make you're playing much better if you practice repeating those three notes at the correct tempo and correct rhythm.

Beginner song #1: The Saints Go Marching In

Listening Sound File #18
Learn the song:
The Saints Go Marching In

https://soundcloud.com/jason_randall/sets/how-to-play-the-fife?utm_source=clipboard&utm_medium=text&utm_campaign=social_sharing

How To Play The Fife

Beginner Song #2: Blue Bells of Scotland

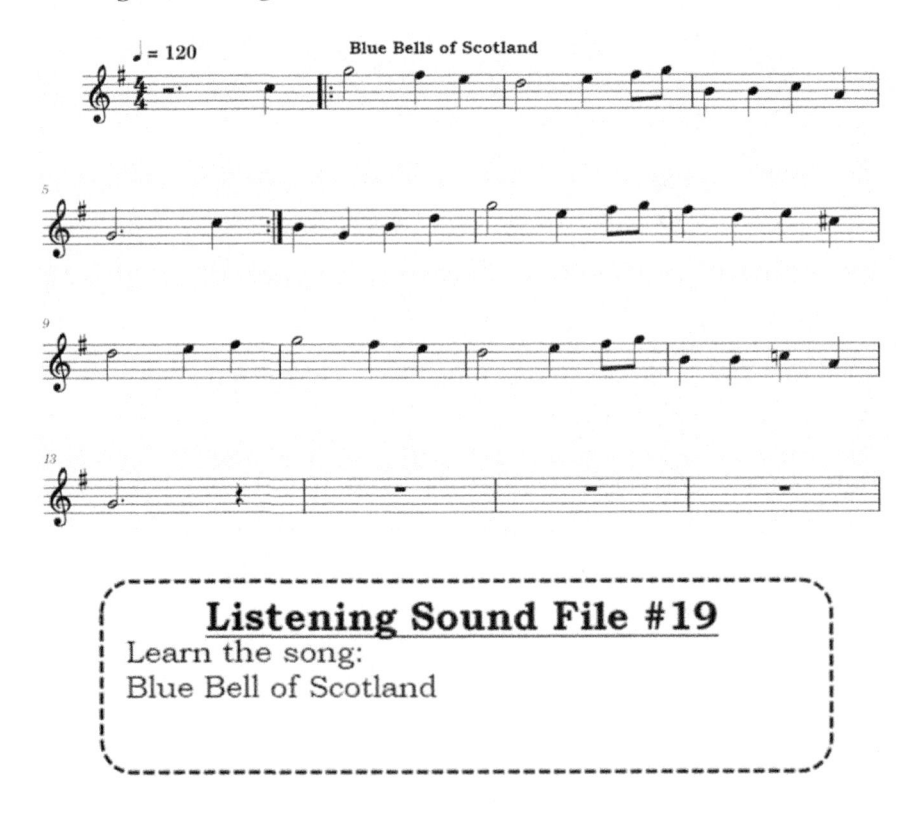

> **Listening Sound File #19**
> Learn the song:
> Blue Bell of Scotland

https://soundcloud.com/jason_randall/sets/how-to-play-the-fife?utm_source=clipboard&utm_medium=text&utm_campaign=social_sharing

Beginner song #3: Ode to Joy

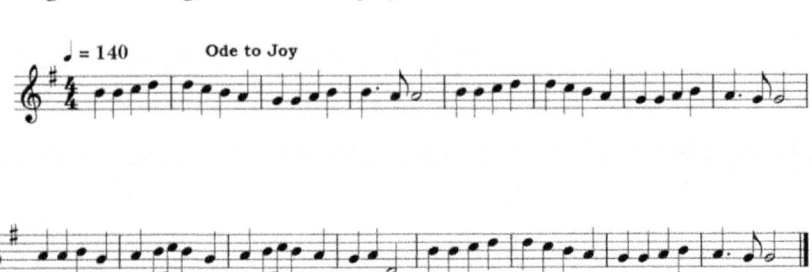

Playing Your First Songs

> **Listening Sound File #20**
> Learn the melody:
> Ode to Joy

https://soundcloud.com/jason_randall/sets/how-to-play-the-fife?utm_source=clipboard&utm_medium=text&utm_campaign=social_sharing

Beginner Song #4: Twinkle, Twinkle Little Star

> **Listening Sound File #21**
> Learn the song:
> Twinkle Twinkle Little Star

https://soundcloud.com/jason_randall/sets/how-to-play-the-fife?utm_source=clipboard&utm_medium=text&utm_campaign=social_sharing

Chapter 6
Intermediate Fife Techniques

Topics Covered:

- Dynamics

- Legato and Staccato

- Triplets

- Trills

- High octave

- Chromatic scale fingering (and D#)

The fife is capable of doing a lot. Intermediate players often never need to play more complicated contemporary pieces because there aren't very many in the repertoire. Having said that, it is possible to achieve more on the instrument, but it usually isn't expected outside of songs that feature difficult speeds.

Dynamics

In music, dynamics is the term for the loudness of an orchestra or instrument. The fife can achieve excessively loud and shrill noises, but it can also be used to convey subdued notes in the lower range. Practice changing these dynamics to fulfill expressional needs. How quietly can you play the fife with a pure tone? How loudly can you play without becoming extravagant? Practice slowly increasing the dynamics across different melody lines. Well-controlled dynamics give much more vibrance to a song.

Sometimes, crescendos or decrescendos show these changes in dynamics. As well, dynamics are marked with certain notations.

pp	Pianissimo	Very soft
p	Piano	Soft
mp	Mezzo-piano	Medium soft
mf	Mezzo-forte	Medium Loud
f	Forte	Loud
ff	Fortissimo	Very Loud
<	Crescendo	Gradually Louder
>	Decrescendo	Gradually Softer

Legato and Staccato

Notes can be articulated differently. Legato is the term that means notes are long and smooth. These notes feel connected and the transition between notes is not articulated. To play legato, fifers usually use the same breath to get through all the notes.

Staccato is much different. These notes are short bursts that last as briefly as possible. When playing staccato, each note gets its own burst of air, clearly defining the beginning and end of the note.

Staccato

Legato

> **Listening Sound File #22**
> Hear the difference between staccato and legato.

https://soundcloud.com/jason_randall/sets/how-to-play-the-fife?utm_source=clipboard&utm_medium=text&utm_campaign=social_sharing

Triplets

Rhythm can become much more complicated than counting a 4/4 or a 3/4. Naturally, time can be divided in myriad ways. Most music tends to favor dividing it in half, like an eighth note being half the value of a quarter note. However, there are other ways to divide the time within one note.

A triplet is the most commonly used, and fifers will see it often. Triplets mean that one note is divided by three parts. Whereas two eighths take equal time to fill one quarter note, it takes three triplet eighths to fill the same exact note time.

♩ = 120

1/8 triplets

1/16 triplets

Triplets are more difficult to count. Most musicians say "trip-uh-let" to count these. The difficulty is making sure the notes take up the right amount of time. Playing faster triplets is much easier than playing slow triplets because there is less margin for error in time allocation. The most recognizable use of triplets is on drum fills in any popular rock or pop song. Usually, but not always, drum rolls speed up based on triplet subdivisions to create rhythmic momentum. It's an easy way to get more notes in at equal time. Since it's a popular percussive technique, the fife will see triplets plenty of times in intermediate sheet music. Practice tapping along to these triplets. As a fifer, you'll play the slower triplets, but practice tapping the faster ones to gain an understanding of how the time is subdivided. The "L" and "R" mean left hand and right hand respectively. You'll notice triplets change which hand is emphasizing the on-beat note. First right, then left.

Intermediate Fife Techniques

[Musical notation: ♩ = 100, with sticking pattern RLR LR LRLR L R L | RLR LR LRLR L R L in triplets]

> **Listening Sound File #23**
> Listen and tap along to some fast triplets at tempo 100.

https://soundcloud.com/jason_randall/sets/how-to-play-the-fife?utm_source=clipboard&utm_medium=text&utm_campaign=social_sharing

Trills

Another intermediate technique is the ability to play trills. Trills are a fun one. They are the quick succession of alternating notes between the main note and the next note up in the scale. This means that in the D major scale, a trill on the note "D" would be bouncing between D and E. The trill on F# would be F# to G in quick succession. Consider these two examples. The note D to the note E has two steps between them. D to D#, then up to E. We do not play the D#, only the D and E. But F# to G has only one step. These are both trills because they are the next note in the scale, but the difference between the note distance is not the same. D to E is what musicians call a major second, while F# to G is what musicians call a minor second. Try both, and see how the color of their changing tones sounds different.

To see the fingering for trills, notice the "*tr*" above the empty hole. The corresponding hole will be quickly covered and uncovered in the same breath. Breath does not cause the trill. The finger blocking and unblocking the specific hole allows the note to change smoothly.

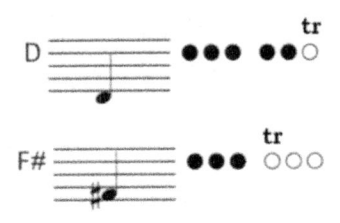

> **Listening Sound File #24**
> Hear two types of trills. In D major, a D trill is a major second and an F# trill is a minor second.

https://soundcloud.com/jason_randall/sets/how-to-play-the-fife?utm_source=clipboard&utm_medium=text&utm_campaign=social_sharing

Several trills are achievable on the fife, and they can really add flair to your music. Practice playing these trills.

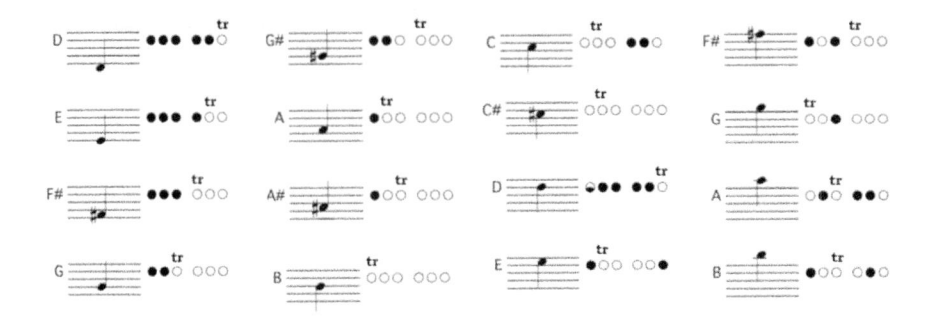

Chromatic Fingering Chart

In music, the term chromatic means it includes every standardized note available. The D major scale has seven note degrees. However, in the standard western division of frequencies, there are 11 notes. These 11 notes are the chromatic scale. Playing them in order has no musical context without harmony or rhythm, while major scales always sound musical.

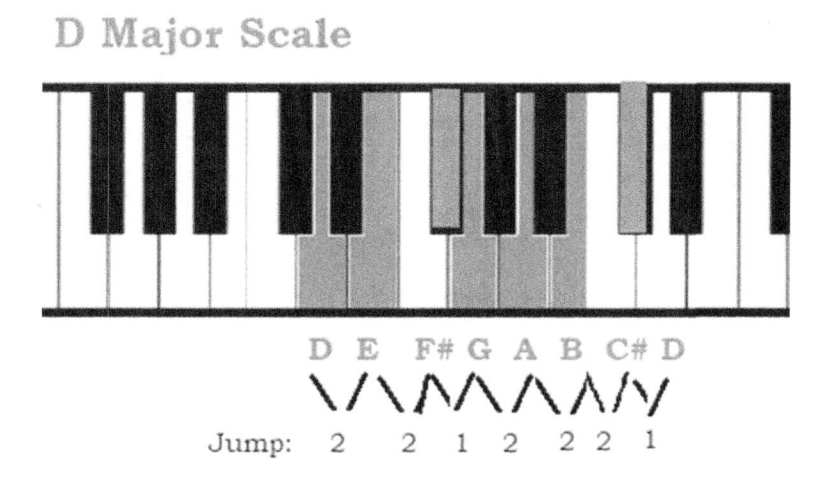

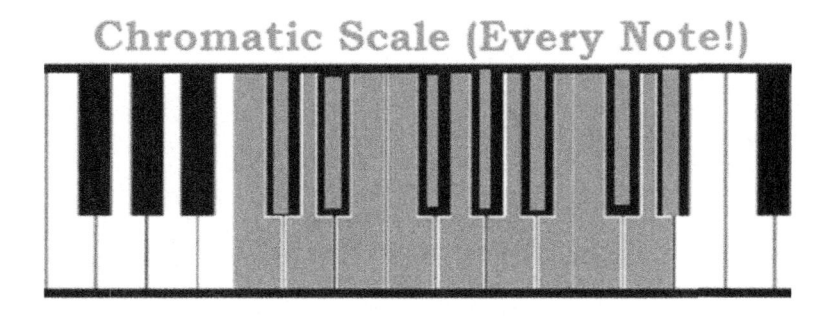

D Major Scale

D E F# G A B C# D

Jump: 2 2 1 2 2 2 1

Chromatic Scale (Every Note!)

Jump 1 every time

How To Play The Fife

The fife is capable of playing every chromatic note within its three octaves. However, the most difficult to play are the low and middle D#s. On a traditional 6-hole fife, this note can only be achieved by half-covering the last hole. It means this note will usually be out of tune. Unless you want to become a master fifer, it may be best to avoid this note.

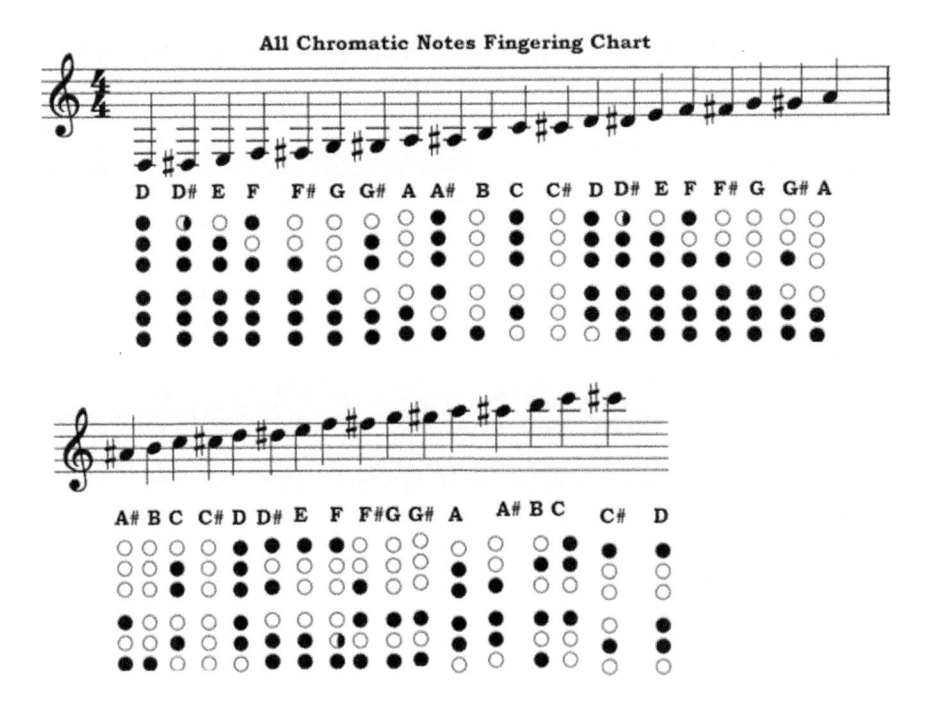

All Chromatic Notes Fingering Chart

Playing the Highest Octave

Previously, you saw how to change between high and low notes by attenuating the angle of breath on the blowhole. You can adjust your jaw and embouchure to achieve this. However, the highest octave is still a challenge. There are several things to consider when trying to reach this octave. One is that the amount of air will be the same. You aren't trying to breathe out more air, but simply breathe out with more of your muscles in your diaphragm. A well-known practice is to stand without your fife. Place your hands on your belly and practice saying "ha" at different volumes. Change the dynamics of your "ha" to get a "ha-AH!" Your body should become tighter and your hand should feel the firmness in your belly without much change in the air you're breathing out.

Another consideration is the windpipe. Make sure you aren't tightening your throat to achieve these higher notes. The windpipe should still be as open as it is for the lower notes. Lastly, the control for your embouchure for these higher notes is in the center of the mouth, not the edges. Focus on the muscles around your philtrum, not at the corners of your mouth.

A Note on Concertos

Composers often write music with the purpose of exploring techniques and pushing the boundaries of how musicians perform. Concertos are pieces of music where a specific instrument is featured. While no concertos have been written for the fife, there are volumes of flute concertos dating from Renaissance to contemporary compositions. In addition, the piccolo has an extensive number of concertos. Since the fife is the original piccolo, these concertos might show more insight on what the instrument is capable of.

Chapter 7
Conclusion - Bringing It All Together

Playing the fife can be a way to express yourself, a skill to be proud of, or a doorway to learning various instruments. If you master the fife, it is easy to segue to other woodwinds, most especially the flute or piccolo. Music tames the beast, as they say. No matter the reason for playing the fife, the more in-tune you become with your instrument, the more you'll feel an indefinable fulfillment and meditative connection.

Composers and performers are continually pushing the boundaries of music, whether it is rhythm, harmony, context, or any other facet of composition. Your journey with the fife may lead you to more expert ventures. Here are some resources to facilitate a jumping-off point into deeper techniques.

Resources:

- Fingering charts
- More traditional fife music
- Tuner
- Fife websites

Fingering Charts

The fingering chart will be the main focus as you begin. And memorizing each finger arrangement will be a matter of practicing often enough. A full chart can be found at these locations:

- https://vvfdc.org/Sheet%20Music/Fife/Fifers%20Booklet.pdf

- https://beafifer.com/fingering.htm

Find whatever chart is easiest to read and practice playing sequences of notes until you memorize them.

More Traditional Fife Music

There are plenty of traditional fife songs. Remember, it's not only about learning, but also creatively exploring.

- http://www.fifedrum.org/excelsior/tunes.shtml

This site has sheet music for many traditional American fife songs. Some of them can get quite difficult in speed or rhythm, which can be the next step to becoming a fife expert.

Tuner

A tuner is an excellent idea to make sure you're playing in tune. It can also be a way to find the natural pitch of your fife, since so many fifes are made in different keys nowadays. While there are various options for tuners in stores, there are also some free online apps.

- TE Tuner & Metronome

- insTuner

- Chromatic Tuner

Fife Websites

It may be difficult to find online communities strictly about the fife, but there are a few that still like to provide tips, songs, and information.

- http://www.fifedrum.org/fifes/

- https://beafifer.com

As a new, fully-fledged fifer, your journey shouldn't stop here. Whether you find marching bands to play with, practice your own precision with the instrument, or simply use it as an escape to enjoy the simple connection to one of the oldest types of instruments known to humankind, you're sure to have a fulfilling pastime.

Unlock Your Musical Potential: Get 30% Off the Next Step in Your Instrumental Journey

As a token of appreciation for your dedication, we're excited to offer you an **exclusive 30% discount** on your next product when you sign up below with your email address.

Click the link below:
https://bit.ly/40NikR2
OR
Use the QR Code:

Unlocking your musical potential is easier with ongoing guidance and support. Join our community of passionate musicians to elevate your skills and stay updated with the latest tips and tricks.

By signing up, you'll also receive our periodic newsletter with additional insights and resources to enhance your musical journey.

Your privacy is important to us. We won't spam you, and you can unsubscribe anytime.

Don't miss out on this opportunity to continue your musical journey with this special discount. Sign up now, and let's embark on this musical adventure together! 𝄞

Printed in Great Britain
by Amazon